# The First-Timer's Guide to Magic Tricks

By Shawn McMaster
Illustrated by Janise Gates

LOWELL HOUSE JUVENILE

LOS ANGELES

NTC/Contemporary Publishing Group

*To my wife, Theresa, for knowing I was going to be a professional magician and marrying me anyway. And for the two wonderful daughters she has given me, with whom I can share this book.*

*—S.M.*

Published by Lowell House
A division of NTC/Contemporary Publishing Group, Inc.
4255 West Touhy Avenue, Lincolnwood (Chicago), Illinois 60646-1975 U.S.A.

Managing Director and Publisher: Jack Artenstein
Director of Publishing Services: Rena Copperman
Editorial Director: Brenda Pope-Ostrow
Editor: Joanna Siebert
Designer: Treesha Runnells Vaux

Lowell House books can be purchased at special discounts
when ordered in bulk for premiums and special sales.
Contact Customer Service at the address above,
or call 1-800-323-4900.

Printed and bound in the United States of America

Library of Congress Catalog Card Number: 99-73105

ISBN: 0-7373-0229-1

RCP 10 9 8 7 6 5 4 3 2 1

# Contents

# To Parents

**M**agic is a wonderful hobby that is enjoying a great amount of renewed interest in recent years. It differs as a hobby from, for example, coin or stamp collecting, as it can help build your child's coordination, dexterity, and self-confidence. By encouraging your child to learn about magic, not only are you satisfying an interest in gadgets and their secret manipulation, but you also are giving your child a way of "pulling one over on the adults." That ability can make a kid feel pretty powerful and encourage more study.

Be supportive when viewing your child's magic tricks. If you are genuinely fooled, by all means *tell* your child that. If, however, you happen to see something you shouldn't have, point this out to your child in a positive manner, and encourage her to work on the trick so that the next time you see it you will be fooled.

Avoid putting your child in the awkward position of telling you how a trick is done. Magic is an art made up of secrets, and the number-one rule of a magician is to never reveal those secrets. It is OK as a spectator to be amazed and exclaim, "How did you do that?"—giving your child a chance to smile and say, "A magician never tells."

Some of the tricks in this book require setup before they can be performed. Your child may ask for your assistance in preparing some of the things needed. All of the materials required are simple household objects or can be bought in any grocery or drugstore. You do not need to hunt down a magic shop to acquire any of these props.

If your child does approach you for assistance in setting up a trick, simply help with the immediate task. Resist the temptation to question your child about the trick. Work with him to get the required setup done, and then let your child fool you when actually performing the trick. It will be more fun that way for both of you!

Your child may ask for your help while creating a costume. Encourage creativity! Offer ideas that will inspire your child to be original. Go through closets together and let your child know which items she may borrow.

You can encourage your child's interest by helping him to find other books on magic. A trip to the library can be very exciting when your child is about to discover new secrets. If possible, help your child search the Internet for more information on magic.

For a special occasion, take your child to a local magic show. She will learn a lot just by watching an accomplished magician. Visit a nearby magic shop together when you have the chance. Allow your child to discover as much as possible about the world of magic.

# HOW TO USE THIS BOOK

The magic tricks in this book are fun and safe to do. Instructions are kept as simple as possible. This sample trick points out the many ways your child will learn about magic.

**Brief description introduces the magic trick**

**Key words encourage independent learning**

**Type of trick being described**

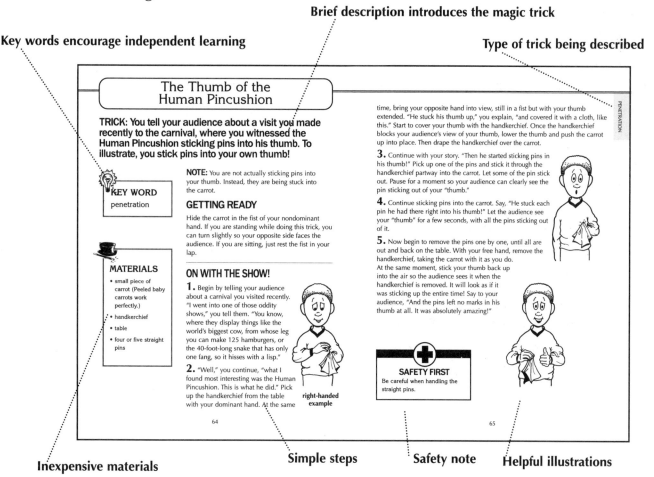

**Inexpensive materials**

**Simple steps**

**Safety note**

**Helpful illustrations**

# The Sneakiest Hobby of Them All

So you want to become a magician, huh? Great! Magic is a wonderful hobby that can teach you some pretty cool things. You'll be able to amaze your friends and make them think you're some kind of wonder-worker.

Magic has been around for thousands of years, and some of its secrets are just as old. This book will introduce you to some of those secrets, along with some newer ones. Use them wisely—and guard them carefully—and soon you will become the talk of the neighborhood.

When people learn that you are a magician, they will naturally ask you to show them a trick or two. This book will supply you with more than enough tricks to perform for them. Try out a few of each kind and see which ones you like best.

Once you master the tricks in this book, you can continue your study of magic by visiting your library and learning other magic secrets, adding those to the ones you already know. The more you study and learn, the sooner you may be able to start creating your own tricks!

Magic is fun, yes. But it is also a serious art form and should be taken seriously. It will take some work to get the tricks just right. Each trick *must* be practiced until it looks right.

When you do put the proper amount of work into magic, it can be a very rewarding experience and offer you many years of fun, too! As a matter of fact, many of today's top magicians first became interested in magic when they were around *your* age!

This book not only provides you with many different tricks to learn, it also offers you tips on creating the art of magic: how to choose the right kind of trick to perform, how to make your tricks seem more magical, and how to dress the part of a magician—everything you need to get started. Study these things as closely as you study the tricks themselves!

# THE KIND OF MAGIC THAT'S RIGHT FOR YOU

The type of tricks you'll perform depends on many things, the most important of which is your interest. Do you want to do small-scale tricks for small groups, maybe while sitting around a table? Or do you have bigger things in mind, like becoming the next David Copperfield and presenting dramatic, even downright spooky mysteries on stage? It's all a matter of your choice and your imagination.

## CLOSE-UP MAGIC

Close-up magic is the style of magic where the tricks are presented on a small scale, using hand props, such as decks of cards, coins or dollar bills, pencils, pens, and that sort of thing.

These tricks are usually performed right under the spectators' noses. They amaze people who aren't used to seeing magic this close. Most people have only seen magicians at a distance, either on a stage or on television. That distance tends to separate them from the magic.

In close-up magic, the spectator is, indeed, right up close to the magician. Sometimes the magic happens in the spectator's own hands! This can have a powerful impact on someone who has watched magic only from afar.

## PARLOR MAGIC AND STAGE MAGIC

These are the types of magic most people have seen, if they have seen a professional magic show at all. Parlor magic and stage magic generally use assistants and bigger props than are used in close-up magic, and they sometimes include music and dramatic lighting. (Don't worry—you will not need any special lighting or music to do the tricks taught in this book!)

Parlor magic and stage magic differ in the space where the magic is presented and the props used. Think of parlor magic as "big close-up magic" or "small stage magic"—as sort of a bridge between close-up and stage magic. Be prepared for some close-up tricks that are big enough to be seen by more than just an intimate audience. Although these tricks can be done from a stage, they do not involve complicated props. The term *parlor* indicates where these tricks were first performed: in someone's parlor or living room.

Stage magic, as suggested by the name, is usually performed on a stage. These are the big illusions you see on television: the floating ladies, the disappearing elephants, the appearing helicopters. Such tricks must be presented in a large space simply because of their size. Don't try bringing an elephant into your friend's living room!

## THE DIFFERENT KINDS OF MAGIC TRICKS

There are many, many different magic tricks—many more than the ones in this book. But all of them, including the ones in this book, will fall into one or more of the categories below.

- ➤ **PRODUCTION** The magician causes someone or something to appear from nowhere.

- ➤ **VANISH** Someone or something disappears into thin air.

- ➤ **TRANSPOSITION** An object or a person magically moves to another location; or, two different objects or people magically switch places.

- ➤ **TRANSFORMATION** Someone or something magically changes into someone or something else.

- ➤ **LEVITATION** The magician causes an object or a person to float in the air with no visible means of support.

- ➤ **SUSPENSION** The magician causes someone or something to balance or hang at an angle that defies gravity.

- ➤ **PENETRATION** Two solid objects magically pass through each other without either of them being destroyed.

- ➤ **RESTORATION** The magician cuts or tears something and then magically puts it back together.

- **MENTALISM** Someone is able to read another person's mind or predict that something will happen before it happens. (Some people who perform mentalism call themselves mentalists rather than magicians, and the tricks they perform, experiments. This type of magic is usually presented very seriously.)

- **ESCAPES** The magician is able to break out of restraints or escape from confinement. (Sorry, but you will not be learning any "escapology" from this book!)

- **BETCHAS** The magician challenges her volunteer to perform some feat, and demonstrates how it can be done after the volunteer fails.

So, as you can see, there are many types of magic you can perform. And you do not have to pick just one! Some magicians perform both close-up and stage magic. Many present a few tricks from each category in their act. It is all up to you and what you feel comfortable doing.

## BE ORIGINAL!

Once you have decided what kind of magic you want to perform, you must decide how you want to perform that magic. Are you going to present yourself as a serious conjurer of ancient mysteries, or are you going to be a comical wizard that weaves fun and laughs into his tricks? Think about it.

Don't get discouraged if the first idea you come up with for a character does not fit you. Some of the best ideas originally started out as something completely different. Keep working at it and you will soon come up with a character that suits you.

Watch other magicians. Don't copy them, but instead ask yourself what it is you admire about that magician. What does she do that you like? What don't you like about the magician? Use your answers to these questions to develop your own style.

The magicians you study have put many years of thought and work into their characters. Once you have decided on your own character, you, too, will have years to develop and refine it.

Always try to be original. When you learn a new trick, including the ones in this book, try to change it around to fit your own character style. Say things the way your character would say them, not the way you saw another magician say it or the way it is written word for word in this book. The more original thinking you put into your magic, the more fresh and pleasing it will be to watch.

# PRESENT YOURSELF WITH CONFIDENCE

A magician is a person of mystery. Whether male or female, serious or funny, he or she is someone who knows how to do things that most people cannot. There is an image people have when they think of a magician, and it is your job to keep that image alive in their minds. You can do that by being well groomed as well as well practiced with your tricks and confident when performing them.

The more professional you appear, the more command you will have over your magic tricks and therefore your audiences. Poor grooming can take away from the audience's enjoyment of watching your magic tricks. Think about how you will appear to the spectators. Are you neatly dressed? If you are wearing a costume, is it in good shape?

The clothes you wear should be clean and free of holes. In general, boys should wear a jacket and maybe a tie, and girls should wear a nice pants outfit or dress. In either case, if you are performing close-up magic tricks, the more pockets you have the better. You can keep many of your props right with you in those pockets.

Of course, you should wear whatever is appropriate for the character you are playing. Look around your home for items to use in your costume, or you might be able to find different pieces of your outfit for very little cost in thrift stores.

Be sure your hair is combed and your teeth are brushed. And, most important, make certain your fingernails and hands are clean. Your fingernails should be neatly trimmed. Your hands are the most visible part of your body when performing magic, so be sure they are clean and presentable at all times.

Getting these things right is just as important as learning and practicing your magic tricks. It is all a part of your presentation.

## PRACTICE MAKES PERFECT

Have you ever heard the phrase "Practice makes perfect"? It is especially true when discussing magic. Not one magic trick in existence can be performed right off the bat. Some are easier than others, but *all* must be practiced. They must be practiced until their actions become natural to you, until you can do the trick without wondering what comes next or worrying whether it will work right. A trick will work right when you put the right amount of practice into it.

It cannot be emphasized enough: The more you practice, the easier the tricks will become and the more confident you will be in doing them. That confidence will come across in your performance and you will appear to be in control. The more confident you feel about the tricks you are performing, the more in command of your audience you will be. Never perform a trick until you are sure of exactly how to do it.

A good place to practice is in front of a mirror. When you perform a magic trick in front of a mirror, you get to see the trick as your audience would. Watch your movements to find out if you can see anything you shouldn't be seeing. For example, if you are holding a box with something hidden in it, make sure you cannot detect the secret object until the time comes to reveal it. If you do see something in the mirror that you shouldn't, chances are your audience would be able to see it as well. That means . . . more practice!

Another good place to practice is in front of a video camera. The video camera captures your performance on tape and allows you to watch it over and over. It also allows you to slow down or pause the tape right where you may be experiencing difficulties. By examining and reexamining the tape, you can pinpoint exactly where a problem in the trick is occurring and how to solve it. Don't you feel lucky? This technology was not available to the great magicians of the past!

Here is a step-by-step guide for learning and practicing every trick in this book:

1. Read the instructions carefully to be sure you understand the trick. Try doing the actions as you read about them.

2. Once you can do the trick from memory (without reading the instructions), practice the trick over and over, either in front of a mirror or for the video camera, and pay close attention to your movements. Work on any problem areas.

3. Once you have gotten the steps and the movements down to a smooth working form, decide how to present the trick to your audience. Think up a script of some sort that you can follow when you perform the trick.

4. Now, costume and all, rehearse the trick as you would perform it before an audience. Pretend they are there. Look at "them" and say your lines. Just as in Step 2, do this bit of rehearsal in front of a mirror or video camera. Rehearse until you are comfortable with your presentation.

5. Go out and knock 'em dead!

## MISDIRECTION

Misdirection can be one of your most important tools as a magician. It not only helps you accomplish some of your tricks but in most cases helps you appear more magical! Misdirection is the practice of diverting the eye—and mind—of your spectator or audience. Here are some examples of how you can use misdirection in your magic:

➤ Make all your moves look natural. Any unnatural actions (doing something in an odd or strange sort of way) will bring attention to you. Quick actions will do the same thing, so don't be in a hurry to get the sneaky part over with. The more normal and natural your actions seem, the less your audience will suspect.

➤ Look where you want the audience to look. If an object is supposed to be in your hand, direct your eyes to that hand (even if there is nothing in it). Your audience's eyes will follow yours.

➤ Give your spectator something to do. While he or she is busy doing what you asked, you can accomplish the sneaky stuff without detection.

Every trick is different and therefore has its own unique opportunities for misdirection to strengthen it. Experiment with your audiences while you are performing your tricks and see what "fakes them out" the most. Keep what works and change what doesn't. The more you use misdirection, truly, the more amazing your magic will become!

## THE "RULES" OF MAGIC

Here are a couple of things that all magicians, amateur or professional, must always remember. Think of them as "magic rules."

First, never repeat the same trick for the same audience. If the audience were to see the exact same trick twice, they might be able to figure it out. Why? Because the first time, the trick caught them by surprise. When you repeat it, they have an opportunity to watch your movements, not the trick itself. Watching your every move, they may be able to catch *you* at making the trick happen. Now, if there is another way of doing the trick, go ahead and do it that way. Then, while the audience will be expecting one thing, you will be doing another. They will be thrown off guard and fooled again!

Second, and most important, never, under any circumstances, tell someone how you did a trick! Magic consists of secrets. These secrets are what make the tricks work and what make it all look like magic. When you tell someone how you did a trick, it will no longer seem so special and mysterious, and you run the risk of seeming like a simple prankster—not a mysterious wonder-worker. Keep the mystery in magic. Don't tell its secrets!

## SOME FINAL WORDS OF ADVICE

Congratulations—you've made it this far! What follows are different magic tricks from the many branches of magic we've discussed. There are even a few optical illusions thrown in for fun. If you skipped the first part of this book to jump right in and learn a few tricks, fine. But please don't perform any trick until you have read the book's introduction.

Some tricks may not fit your personality—skip those. Instead, find ones that do fit you or your character and that you will enjoy performing. Once you have decided on the tricks you would like to perform, begin practicing them. Focus your energy on mastering one trick at a time. Once you have mastered a trick, you will be ready to show it to people—and also to begin learning a new trick.

Remember, some of the tricks are designed to be performed close-up while others are parlor- or stage-type tricks. Do not try doing the close-up tricks for a huge audience. The props will be hard for them to see and the trick will lose its impact. And, of course, don't try performing a big stage trick for one or two people.

Some tricks rely on choosing a volunteer or two from the audience to help out. Choose someone who seems to be having fun watching your magic. Don't ever force anyone to help out who doesn't want to. It will be a difficult and awkward situation for both of you. Also, don't ever make fun of, embarrass, or try to appear better than a volunteer. It should be a fun experience for everyone: you, your audience, and the volunteer.

Good luck, and have fun!

---

### NOTE

**To keep the instructions simple, we use the terms *dominant* and *nondominant* throughout the book. Your dominant hand is the hand you normally use for writing. If you are right-handed, your right hand is your dominant hand and your left hand is your nondominant hand. If you are left-handed, your left hand is your dominant hand and your right hand is your nondominant hand. Some of the illustrations have been labeled to show which hand is dominant in the trick.**

---

# This Is Mind Reading?!

**TRICK: You "mentally" send a word to a volunteer. Well . . . sort of!**

## KEY WORDS

clairvoyance
ESP
mentalism

## MATERIALS

- pencil
- pad of paper

## ON WITH THE SHOW!

**1.** Choose a volunteer, then tell him that you are going to send a simple word from your mind into his. Act very serious about this. Tell your volunteer to clear his mind so that he will be more receptive.

**2.** Write the word *NO* in big letters on the pad, but don't allow anyone to see what you have written. Concentrate on your volunteer for a few moments.

**3.** After you have "sent your thought," ask your volunteer, "Do you have any idea what I have just written on my pad?" Of course, your volunteer will say no. As soon as he says this, act very surprised and turn your pad around for all to see. "Yes! That is excellent!" you exclaim.

## FIRST-TIMER'S TIP!

**This is a groaner of a joke disguised as a magic trick. The more you "sell" it, though, the funnier it will be to your audience. Act serious right up to the moment you reveal the word. Then be sure to follow with a really good magic trick to make up for this joke of a one.**

# Reading Without Looking at the Words

**TRICK: You are able to tell your audience details about a page randomly chosen from a book.**

## KEY WORDS

memory

mentalism

## MATERIALS

- pad of paper
- pencil
- book

## GETTING READY

To prepare, familiarize yourself with two pages—pages 10 and 89—from the book you will use in the trick. You must remember a few important details about each page, such as titles, pictures, or anything that stands out. Don't get the two pages mixed up!

## ON WITH THE SHOW!

**1.** Ask for two volunteers to help you with this trick. Make sure they are old enough to perform the tasks. Hand one volunteer a pad of paper and a pencil. Hand the other volunteer the book. To the first volunteer you say, "I would like you to think of a three-digit number. To make it difficult, make all three digits different." This is a fib. This doesn't make the trick difficult—it makes the trick work!

**2.** After your first volunteer says the number he has chosen, tell him to write it down on the pad.

**3.** "Now," you say, "reverse that number and make a subtraction problem out of it. For example, if you chose the number 723, reverse it to become 327. Then subtract 327 from 723. Get it?"

**4.** Your volunteer does the math and tells you when he is done. "Now," you say, "I want you to reverse the total you just came up with, and add the total and the reversed total together."

**5.** Your volunteer lets you know when the math is done. His total should be 1,089. In fact, as long as your volunteer follows your instructions and does the math right, the total will always be 1,089! You now know the number your volunteer has written on the pad, but you must not let on that you do.

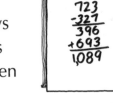

```
  723
 -327
  396
 +693
 1,089
```

**6.** "Look at the number you now have on paper. How many digits does it have?" you ask. "Four," your volunteer replies. "All right, cut the number in half so that you have two 2-digit numbers," you instruct him. "What are the two numbers?" Your volunteer answers that they are 10 and 89—the numbers of the same two pages you memorized before the trick began!

**7.** Tell your volunteer to pick one of those numbers. Let's say he picks 89. Instruct the volunteer who is holding the book to turn to page 89 and look at the page. Concentrate for a minute, then begin to describe what is on page 89. Your audience will be astonished!

## FIRST-TIMER'S TIP!

Make sure your volunteer tells you the number he has chosen at the beginning of the trick. If your volunteer forgets to make all three digits different, politely say, "Make this difficult for me and make all three digits different." Your volunteer will then choose a number that will work. If your volunteer does the math incorrectly, go ahead and describe both pages 10 and 89. Your volunteer will state that you are wrong. Look confused and say, "I don't understand. Those are the images that I received. Are you sure you did the math right?" At that point, your volunteer will double check the math, find his or her mistake and correct it, then discover you were right all along!

## BRAIN BUSTER

This trick works best if all three digits of the original number are different. Why? What would happen if the number picked at the beginning of the trick were 757? How about 222? Would a number like 551 or 799 work? Try the problem with these numbers and find out which ones work and which ones don't, and why.

17

# A Drop in the Hat

**TRICK: You place a hat on the floor and bet a volunteer that you can drop more cards into the hat than she can. Your volunteer tries, and then you try. You always win!**

## KEY WORDS

air

"betcha"

gravity

## MATERIALS

- hat
- deck of cards

## ON WITH THE SHOW!

**1.** Place a hat upside down on the floor. Hand the deck of cards to your volunteer and ask her to stand near the hat. "Try to get as many cards as you can into the hat by dropping them one by one from waist level," you tell her. Most likely, your friend will try to do this by holding each card vertically, or upright. When cards are dropped from this position, they flutter in all directions. Some may fall into the hat, but the amount will be small.

**2.** Once the entire deck has been used up, count the number of cards your friend has successfully dropped into the hat.

**3.** Now it is your turn. Gather all the cards together and take your position near the hat. Hold each card horizontally, or flat, grasping it by the edges, over the hat. Drop all the cards from this position, with your hand no lower than at waist level. Dropped this way, almost every one will fall straight down toward the floor and into the hat!

## FIRST-TIMER'S TIP!

The power of suggestion is an important part of magic. You can make it more likely that your volunteer will drop the cards the "wrong" way with a simple move. When you begin your challenge, casually take one of the cards and hold it vertically, not horizontally, above the hat as you are describing what you want your volunteer to do. While your volunteer is listening and watching, she will observe you holding the card in a vertical position. When the deck is handed to her, your volunteer will probably hold the cards in that position, too— even though you never specified the cards had to be held that way!

# The See-Through Hand

**TRICK: With the help of an optical illusion, you cause your friends to see holes in the center of their hands.**

### KEY WORDS
optical illusion

## MATERIALS

- construction paper
- glue
- sequins
- colored markers
- cardboard tube from paper towel or toilet paper roll

## GETTING READY

Using construction paper, glue, sequins, and colored markers, decorate the cardboad tube to make it look magical.

## ON WITH THE SHOW!

**1.** Tell your friends it is a little-known fact that every human hand has a hole in it. It is not easy to locate, but you can find it using your magic tube.

**2.** Demonstrate how they may see the hole. Hold the tube in your nondominant hand so you will be able to look through it like a telescope.

**3.** Open your other hand so it is upright, palm facing you, and touch it to the tube halfway down. (The pinkie side of that hand should be touching the tube.)

**4.** Now, keeping the tube and hand in the same position, move them toward your face. Keep both eyes open, and place the tube against your eye (the left eye if you're right-handed, the right eye if you're left-handed). As you look through the tube, your eyes will adjust, and it will appear as if there is a big hole in the middle of your palm and that you are looking through it!

**5.** Say, "With this magic it's easy to see the hole in your hand. I'm looking at mine right now!" Offer the tube to one of your friends so that he can see the "hole" in his hand. Watch each friend's reaction as he or she takes a turn.

**right-handed
example**

# BRAIN BUSTER

Do you know what an optical illusion is? Can you explain this one? What is causing you to see a "hole" in the center of your hand?

# Squashing the Salt

**TRICK: You magically cause a salt shaker to pass through a solid table.**

## KEY WORDS

penetration

solid

## MATERIALS

- table (with tablecloth) and chair
- salt shaker
- paper napkin

## ON WITH THE SHOW!

**1.** Sitting at a table, show the salt shaker and paper napkin. Tell your audience that every table has a soft spot. "It is just a matter of finding it," you explain. Inform your audience that when you find this particular table's soft spot, you will push the salt shaker right through it.

**2.** Wrap the napkin around the shaker. Be careful as you do this that you don't tear the napkin. Also, be sure the entire salt shaker is covered by the napkin. Then begin moving the wrapped shaker around the surface of the table as if looking for the soft spot.

**3.** Stop and announce that you have found the spot. Hit the top of the wrapped shaker. Don't hurt yourself by hitting too hard—you only have to sharply rap the top. Of course, nothing happens.

**4.** Look confused. "It is more difficult to find the right spot than it would seem," you tell the audience. Move the shaker, still wrapped in the napkin, back toward you and the edge of the table. Examine the spot where the shaker was sitting. Press down on it with your free hand. Shrug and begin moving the salt shaker around the table again.

**5.** Stop at a new spot. Repeat all the movements as before while talking to the audience.

**6.** Again begin moving the shaker around the table. Up until now, you have been pretending to examine the table for soft spots in order to misdirect your audience. You have set them up to expect the same results this time. But now you are going to change things on them, and they will be totally surprised!

**7.** This time, as you stop, announce excitedly that you really think you've found the soft spot. Hit the top of the shaker just as before. Nothing will happen. Move the shaker toward you, just as you have the last couple of times, and examine the table. Allow the wrapped shaker to pass the edge of the table, and the shaker will slip silently out of the napkin into your lap. Make sure your knees are together! The napkin will keep the shape of the shaker, making it appear as if the shaker is still there.

**8.** Act very confused and say, "I can't seem to find the right spot." Pause a second and look at a different part of the table, and then exclaim, "Wait! I think I see it!" Move the napkin (still in the shape of the shaker) to the spot you are examining. Look at your audience and say, "I hope this is it!" As you're speaking, hit the napkin. To the surprise of your audience, it will flatten onto the table. It will appear as if the shaker went right through the table!

**9.** Reach underneath the tablecloth as if you are pulling the salt shaker from the bottom of the table. Secretly grab the shaker from your lap before moving your hands back into view. Show your audience the salt shaker and accept your applause.

## FIRST-TIMER'S TIP!

Make sure you practice this trick in front of a mirror or video camera. The success of this trick depends on what the audience sees—and doesn't see. Be sure the wrapped shaker always stays within the audience's view. Also, hold the wrapped shaker level with the table when you drop the shaker into your lap. If you hold the napkin too high, the audience will see the shaker drop out of it.

# The Bottle and Straw Bamboozle

**TRICK: You challenge someone to pick up a bottle using only a straw and not touching the bottle in any way. The person tries and fails. Only you can do it!**

## KEY WORDS

"betcha"

hook

wedge

## MATERIALS

- small bottle about 7½ to 8 inches high and not too big around

- two nonbendable drinking straws of the same length

## ON WITH THE SHOW!

Do this trick over a soft, flat surface so the bottle won't break if it falls.

**1.** Begin by placing the bottle on a soft, flat surface. Hand your volunteer a straw. Issue the challenge to pick up the bottle without touching it in any way. The bottle can be lifted only by using the straw, nothing else. Your volunteer will probably not be able to do it.

**2.** Now show your audience how it is done. Put the bottle back in its original position if your volunteer moved it. Start by bending one end of a new straw to make a hook.

**3.** Holding on to the other end of the straw, insert the hook into the mouth of the bottle. Allow the hook to pass through the neck of the bottle and into its wider part. At this point, the hook will open out a bit.

24

**4.** Now pull up on the end of the straw you are holding. This will wedge the straw inside the bottle. It should stay wedged tightly enough for you to lift the bottle up into the air!

## FIRST-TIMER'S TIP!

Practice this trick until you know how much of the straw to bend, as well as how and when to pull up on the straw to wedge it in the bottle. Bottles vary in size, and some straws are sturdier than others. Experiment until you find the right combination of bottle and straw.

# Spot the Jack

**TRICK: You instruct a volunteer to rotate one of four jacks 180 degrees (end to end) while your back is turned. Once you have turned back around, you correctly name the turned-around jack.**

## KEY WORDS

asymmetry

mentalism

symmetry

## MATERIALS

- four jacks from the same deck of cards

## GETTING READY

You may have to look through a few decks to find the right one for performing this trick. Every deck of cards is printed a bit differently, and you need a deck with the jacks printed a certain way. That is, the jacks must be slightly off center. In other words, the white border on one side of the picture is a bit wider than on the opposite side. This isn't easily noticed unless you are looking for it. If possible, use Bicycle Rider Back Playing Cards, printed by the U.S. Playing Card Company in Cincinnati, Ohio. They are the most commonly found playing cards in stores and homes around the United States. You also need a table for this trick.

## ON WITH THE SHOW!

**1.** Place the jacks on the table faceup with all the wide borders on the right-hand side of each card. Do not call this to your audience's attention.

**2.** Choose a volunteer, then instruct him to rotate one jack 180 degrees, end to end, while your back is turned. "Make sure that you keep the jack as straight as possible after you've turned it," you say.

**3.** Turn your back so the volunteer can do his part. He should tell you when to turn back around.

**4.** When you turn to face the jacks, look carefully at them. You will notice that three of them still have the wide borders on the right-hand side—but one of them will have a wide border on the left-hand side. That is the one your volunteer turned around. Do not announce that you have found the jack right away. Pick up each card and look at it. After you have built up suspense, correctly name the card that was turned around.

## FIRST-TIMER'S TIP!

If you have a hard time tracking down the proper deck of cards to do this trick, you can use four jacks from any deck, but you must give each of them a special mark that only you can see. This mark can be placed within the picture of the jack itself, but all marks must be in the same location and easily recognized by you. Plus, they must be near one end or in a corner so that when one of the jacks is turned around, the mark is in a different place than in the other three. Use a black or red felt-tipped marker to make your marks. These colors are used most often in the design of the jacks, and a carefully placed dot in one corner will not be noticed.

# All Shook Up!

**TRICK: You magically cause four pennies sealed inside a glass to disappear without a trace.**

## KEY WORDS

momentum

vanish

## MATERIALS

- four pennies
- drinking glass
- handkerchief
- rubber band

## ON WITH THE SHOW!

**1.** Start by placing the pennies in the glass and shaking them around a bit. Your audience will clearly see the coins.

**2.** Next, place the handkerchief over the mouth of the glass. Secure it in place with the rubber band, leaving the handkerchief a little bit loose. You have now sealed the coins inside the glass.

**right-handed example**

**3.** After the cloth is in place, hold the glass with your dominant hand near the bottom so the audience cannot see the coins. Give the coins one more shake to "prove" they are all still there. What you are really doing is giving them a shake upward toward the handkerchief. This may take a little practice, but your aim is to get all four pennies to fly up and over the lip of the glass so they end up hanging just over the lip, on the side of the glass facing you, inside the handkerchief.

**4.** Now move the glass to your nondominant hand. Make sure your hands overlap as you do this, so you don't reveal that the coins are gone. The side of the handkerchief holding the coins should be near, or facing, you, not facing your audience.

**5.** Wave your free hand over the glass and say a magic word or two. Then, using that free hand, grab the cloth. Be sure to grab the coins, too, through the cloth. With the coins securely in your grasp, pluck the handkerchief off the top of the glass and move it away (along with the coins). Be careful as you do this so the coins don't clink together and make a noise.

**6.** Show the audience that the glass is empty, and accept your applause!

## BRAIN BUSTER

Is it possible to make the coins "magically" return? Think about this trick, then figure out a way to do it. Borrow all four of the coins from members of the audience, then write down their dates. Make them vanish; then make all four return to the glass or appear in some other location. Ask an audience member to check the dates to prove that they are the same coins.

## FIRST-TIMER'S TIP!

Your final shake of the coins should not look any different from the shakes you did before. In other words, it should not look like you are trying to get the coins to flip over the lip of the glass. Make sure all your movements look perfectly natural.

# The Bigger and Bigger Bandanna

**TRICK:** You magically cause an ordinary bandanna to grow in length as you twirl it in front of you.

## KEY WORD
transformation

## MATERIALS

• bandanna

## ON WITH THE SHOW!

**1.** Pass the bandanna around to be examined by your audience. Start telling your audience a story. "This bandanna once belonged to a stagecoach robber. The bandanna was too small to mask his face," you say.

**2.** After everyone has had a chance to look over the bandanna and it's been returned to you, position it so you are holding it by diagonal corners, with the fabric hanging in front of you. As you are getting the bandanna into this position, secretly bunch up a bit of cloth in each of your hands. Just a few inches will do. Once this is done, you will be holding the cloth by diagonal corners, with a few inches of fabric balled up in your hands. Tell your audience, "Fortunately, he was also an amateur magician."

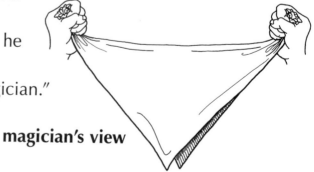

**magician's view**

30

**3.** Begin twirling the bandanna away from you so that it starts to twist up like a rope. Once the bandanna tightens, stop twirling and pull the cloth taut. Now you say, "He made the bandanna grow until it was the perfect size of his face!" As you pull, allow just a tiny bit of fabric to slip out of each hand. It will appear to the audience as if the bandanna magically stretched a little.

**4.** Begin twirling again. When you stop twirling, pull the bandanna taut and let a bit more cloth escape from each hand—the bandanna will again appear to grow!

**5.** Continue this process until you run out of cloth to let slip from your hands. At that point, put the bandanna into your pocket, and take your bow.

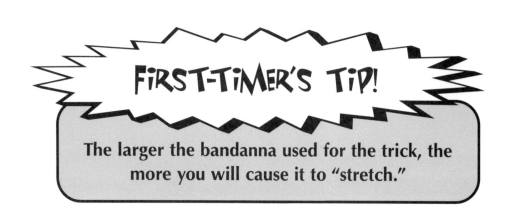

## FiRST-TiMER'S TiP!

The larger the bandanna used for the trick, the more you will cause it to "stretch."

# Those "Touchy" Cards

**TRICK: You lay out some playing cards faceup on the table and ask a volunteer to choose one while your back is turned. When you turn back around, you can name the chosen card.**

## KEY WORDS

code

mentalism

## MATERIALS

- deck of cards
- table

## GETTING READY

Before performing this trick, ask a friend to help you. Your secret helper must pretend to be part of the audience, just like everyone else. You both must remember a secret code or the trick will not work. The secret code is this: Lay out the playing cards in an H pattern on the table. When your back is turned, the first volunteer will touch a card from that layout. Your secret helper will begin to touch each card after you have turned back around. When he reaches the single middle card (the one in the center of the H pattern), he touches that card in a spot that indicates where the chosen card can be found. For example, if the chosen card is in the upper left position in the H pattern, your secret helper touches the upper left-hand corner of the middle card. If the card chosen by your first volunteer is the middle card, then your secret helper must touch the middle card right in the center. Your secret helper must remember to touch the single middle card before he touches the chosen card.

## ON WITH THE SHOW!

**1.** To begin the trick, choose two volunteers. The second volunteer you select must be your secret helper.

**2.** Lay out seven different playing cards faceup on the table. You should lay them out like this: three cards in a vertical line, going straight up and down, then one card to the right of the middle one, then three more cards in a line parallel to the first. When laid out correctly, the pattern of cards should resemble the letter *H*.

**3.** Tell the first volunteer to select a card, once your back is turned, by touching it for everyone to see.

**4.** Once the choice has been made and you have turned back around, instruct the second volunteer (your secret helper) to slowly touch each card in any order he chooses and ask you each time, "Is this the card?"

**5.** Watch carefully as your second volunteer begins to touch the cards one by one. Pay close attention when he touches the middle card using the code described above.

**6.** Once you know the location of the chosen card, wait for your secret helper to touch it and ask, "Is this the card?" When he does, shout out, "Yes! That's it!"

33

# Cunning Currency

## TRICK: You magically balance the end of a dollar bill on your finger.

### KEY WORDS

air pressure

George Washington

suspension

### MATERIALS

- $1 bill (Try to get a new bill. The newer and crisper the bill, the better it works. Get all the bends and kinks out of the bill so that it is perfectly straight.)

## ON WITH THE SHOW!

**1.** You announce to your audience that, although they may not know this, George Washington came from a long line of circus performers. "He used to be able to balance himself on *anything*," you tell them. "Watch," you say as you display a dollar bill. "He will balance on the end of my finger."

**2.** Turn your nondominant hand palm up, and close all your fingers, except the index finger, and thumb into a fist. Leave the index finger extended.

**3.** Stand with your side facing the audience. With your dominant hand, turn the bill so George is "facing" the audience, too. Stand the bill on its short end on the surface of your extended finger, and then let go.

**4.** Believe it or not, the bill will balance on your finger! Keep your hand as steady as possible. (It will take a little practice to keep it balanced.)

**5.** Once George has finished his balancing act, give the bill to someone so it can be examined.

**left-handed example**

**B**RAIN **B**USTER

What causes the bill to stand upright on your finger? Do you know? The air on either side of the bill will be enough to keep it standing upright. But remember, the bill must stand on its short end. What happens when you try to stand the bill on its long end? The trick will not work as well, because there is less bill standing for the air around it to keep it balanced.

# The Sudden Disappearance

**TRICK: You show your audience a dime lying in the palm of your hand. You close your hand, snap your fingers, and open your hand again. The dime is gone!**

## KEY WORDS

vanish

wax

## MATERIALS

- wax
- dime

## GETTING READY

Roll the wax into a small ball and stick it to the nail of the middle finger of your dominant hand. Now you are ready to begin.

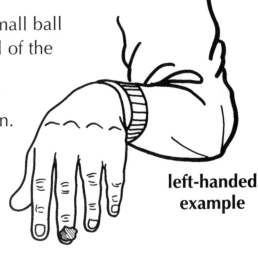

**left-handed example**

## ON WITH THE SHOW!

**1.** Open your dominant hand palm up. Your audience will not see the wax, because it is stuck to the opposite side of your middle finger. With your nondominant hand, show your audience the dime, then place it on the center of your other palm.

**2.** Now close your hand into a fist, turning it palm down. As your hand turns palm down, work your fingertips into the palm of your hand so that the wax comes in contact with the dime. Squeeze a little to make sure the dime sticks to the wax.

**3.** Snap the fingers of your nondominant hand, then start to open the hand you had in a fist. A split second after that hand begins to open, turn it palm up again. Keep all of your fingers together, and the coin will be hidden from view.

## FiRST-TiMER'S TiP!

Timing is very important when performing this trick. You must practice turning your hand palm up and opening your fingers at the right moment. If your timing is right, you will keep the coin out of the audience's view. It may seem hard at first, but once you do it right, you will know exactly how to pull it off every time. You might want to try reversing the trick. In other words, you could magically *produce* a dime. Experiment a little and see what else you can come up with.

# The Pres Says, "Cheese"

**TRICK: You fold a $1 bill in such a way that when your friends look at it, it appears as if George Washington is smiling—and then frowning.**

## KEY WORDS

money

optical illusion

## MATERIALS

- $1 bill (This can really be done with any bill but looks best using a $1, $5, or $50 bill. If possible, use a new bill. Newer bills will hold the folds better than older ones.)

## ON WITH THE SHOW!

**1.** Display the bill for your audience and say, "Now I am going to magically alter the president's face." Hold the bill portrait side up, but in a vertical (up and down) position. Fold part of the bill backward, so the fold line goes through the president's eye and the corner of his mouth. The fold line must be straight. Crease this fold well.

**2.** Turn the bill 180 degrees and make an identical fold through the other eye and corner of the mouth. Your bill is now folded almost in half, with a small flat portion at the center.

**3.** You must now make one more fold. Push down gently in the center of that small flat portion to create a V shape. Crease this fold so the V stays put.

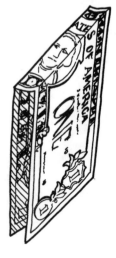

**4.** Now, with the portrait upright and facing you, grip the ends of the bill in each hand and pull open the V fold. Do not pull hard or open it all the way—just gently tug on the ends to open the V slightly.

**5.** Still holding the ends, tilt the bill away from you a bit. Keep staring at the president as you do this. He will appear to smile! The more you tilt the bill away from you, the bigger his smile.

**6.** Now reverse the direction. Start tilting the bill toward you, and watch the president's face as you do. He will gradually stop smiling and begin to frown! Again, the more you tilt the bill, the bigger the frown.

# BRAIN BUSTER

Why do you think the president on the bill appears to smile or frown depending on the way you hold the bill? What causes this optical illusion? Here's another eerie optical illusion you can try. Find a magazine cover featuring a close-up picture of a face. Prop the cover up on a table so that the face is looking right at you. Now, keeping your eyes on the face, begin to move around the room. It will appear as if the eyes are following you!

# Instant Ocean

**TRICK: Using only a few items and a glass of water, you magically create a miniature ocean.**

## KEY WORDS

diffusion

ocean

transformation

## MATERIALS

- salt
- small plastic container (A film canister is perfect.)
- blue food coloring
- two drinking glasses about the same size
- bag (canvas, or a paper grocery bag)
- small piece of seaweed (or a piece of any plant that resembles something you might find in the ocean)
- small plastic fish (or any kind of plastic marine animal toy)

## GETTING READY

**1.** Pour some salt into the plastic container. This will be your "sea salt."

**2.** Pour a little food coloring into the bottom of one of the glasses. Make sure the food coloring does not run down the sides of the glass. (Beforehand, experiment with the amount of food coloring needed to get a deep blue that is not too light or too dark when mixed with the water.) Put the glass into your bag.

**3.** Place all the other items in the bag, too. The second glass stays outside of the bag. Fill it with regular tap water. You are now ready to begin.

## ON WITH THE SHOW!

**1.** "This," you say, holding up the full glass, "is ordinary tap water." You then reach into the bag and remove the container of salt, the seaweed, and the plastic fish.

**2.** "I have been taught an ancient spell that will allow me to create an ocean wherever I want," you say. You then point to the items on the table and continue, "Today's ocean will be a bit small, but I will do my best."

40

**3.** Reach into the bag once again and remove the other drinking glass using your dominant hand. Be careful not to tip the glass so the audience can see the inside. You will not have a hard time concealing the coloring in the bottom of the glass if you hold it near the bottom.

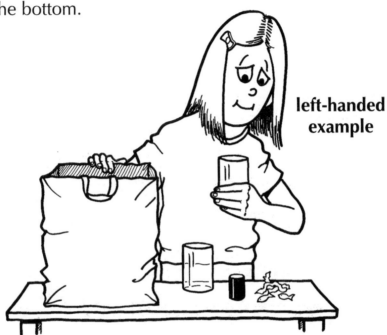

**left-handed example**

**4.** "These are all the elements needed to cast the spell," you say as you begin tossing the items into the "empty" glass with your nondominant hand. "A fish, a little bit of seaweed, and just a pinch of sea salt."

**5.** Once all the items are in the glass, pick up the other (full) glass using the hand that did the tossing. Holding both glasses before you, chant: "With this motion, I create an ocean!" Quickly pour the water into the glass with the items you've tossed in it. You may want to swirl this "ocean" glass in small circles as the water is being poured. This will ensure that the food coloring mixes well with the water. It will appear to everyone watching as if the water magically becomes a deep blue color—and the glass transforms into a miniature ocean, complete with seaweed and fish!

**6.** You may now allow your "ocean" to be examined closely by members of your audience.

## FIRST-TIMER'S TIP!

This trick is open to your imagination. The items included here to create your miniature ocean are only suggestions. You can use whatever kind of marine animals and plants you want. You can make this trick humorous or serious. However, you must always use the blue food coloring. That's what turns the ordinary water into "ocean" water.

# The Box of Answers

**TRICK: An answer to a yes or no question magically appears on a card in an otherwise apparently empty box!**

## KEY WORDS

energy

production

## MATERIALS

- scissors
- two small cardboard boxes about 5 inches square
- white posterboard
- felt pen

## GETTING READY

**1.** First you must construct the special box. Using scissors, cut out the bottom of one of the boxes. Throw the rest of that box away—you will not need it. Trim the piece of cardboard so that it fits easily into the other box. Trimmed properly, it should look like the bottom of the other box when inside it.

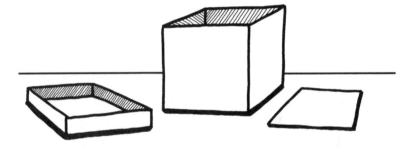

**2.** From the posterboard, cut out two identical 2-by-4½-inch pieces. These will be your cards.

**3.** On one of the small cards, write a message that can be an answer to a yes or no question. Be creative. Write something like "The spirits believe that it will come to pass" or "No way! What are you, CRAZY?!" Leave the other card blank.

**4.** After you have written your response, place this card facedown inside the lid of the box, so your writing is against the lid. Now put the piece of cardboard on top of the card. It won't fit as well as it did in the bottom of the box, but don't worry. It just needs to cover the card. Place the lid to one side, where it will not be the center of attention.

## ON WITH THE SHOW!

**1.** Start the trick by showing that the box is empty. Ask, "Is there anyone in the audience tonight who has a question burning to be answered?" Show your volunteer the blank card, and place it in the box.

**2.** Now carefully slide the lid into position. (You will have to hold everything in place with your fingers as you do so.) Once the lid is on, the secret cardboard piece will fall to the bottom of the box, covering the blank card. The card with your message on it will now be lying on top of the secret cardboard piece. (The piece of cardboard will look just like the bottom of the box.)

**3.** Have your volunteer put her hands on top of the box and ask her question. It must be a question that can be answered with a yes or a no. Tell her to focus her energy on the box.

**4.** As soon as the question has been stated, open the box and peer inside. Look up at your volunteer and say, "I think you've gotten your answer." Take out the card and hand it to your volunteer so that she can read the message that has eerily "appeared" on it!

# FiRST-TiMER'S TiP!

While practicing placing the lid on the box, note whether the secret cardboard piece makes any sound as it drops to the bottom. If it does, make sure you can cover up the sound by talking with your volunteer. You may want to ask a trusted friend or a parent to watch you practice this trick before you perform it for an audience.

# The Eager Jack at Your Service!

**TRICK: With a tap of your hand, the jack of diamonds magically changes into the king of diamonds.**

## KEY WORDS
royalty
transformation

## MATERIALS
• deck of cards

## GETTING READY

**1.** Find the jack of diamonds and the king of diamonds and remove them from the deck.

**2.** Place the jack facedown on top of the deck. Then place the king facedown on top of the jack. The king should be the very top card.

## ON WITH THE SHOW!

**1.** To begin the trick, hold the deck facedown in the palm of your nondominant hand. With your opposite hand, pick up the top two cards as one. This must be done carefully so the cards do not separate. The easiest way to accomplish this is to place your thumb at the short end of the deck closest to you with your fingers at the other end. Then, with your thumb, pull up the top two cards, one by one. Press the two cards together and push them off the top of the deck, keeping them together with the help of your fingers at the other end. Now flip your hand up to show the audience the face of the jack. They will think this is the top card of the deck.

**magician's view**

**(right-handed example)**

**2.** "This card can be considered the prince in the deck of cards," you explain. "You know that princes are always eager to become king. You also know how a prince becomes the king, right?" you ask.

**3.** After the audience has seen the face of the jack, place the cards back on top of the deck facedown. Make sure they stay straight. "The king must either pass away or pass the throne on," you continue as you tap the top of the deck. "Then, and *only* then, does the prince become the king."

**4.** Once you tap the top of the deck, flip up the top card (leaving the jack facedown on the deck), and show your audience that the jack has "magically changed" into the king!

# BRAIN BUSTER

Using the technique of showing two cards as one, what other magic tricks could you perform? What if instead of picking up two cards, you actually picked up three? Four? Figure out a way for your "top" card to change its identity two or three times.

47

# I've Got Your Number!

## TRICK: Your prediction matches the card a volunteer chooses.

**KEY WORD**
mentalism

## MATERIALS

- four cards—the two of clubs, king of diamonds, seven of hearts, and four of spades—from the same deck

- piece of paper

- pencil

- envelope

- table

## GETTING READY

Decide on one of the cards from the four and write its name on the piece of paper. Let's say you decide on the seven of hearts. On the piece of paper, write this sentence: "The volunteer will select the seven of hearts." Fold the paper up and seal it in the envelope. You are now ready to begin the trick.

## ON WITH THE SHOW!

**1.** In a row on the table, lay out the two of clubs, king of diamonds, seven of hearts, and four of spades. Lay the cards out from left to right in front of a volunteer. Make sure that you put the seven of hearts in the third position. This is important!

**2.** Hand the sealed envelope to another volunteer to hold.

**3.** Now comes the fun part!

- You instruct your first volunteer to look at the four cards and then decide on one. "Touch the one you choose," you tell him. Believe it or not, most people will naturally choose the card that is in the third position! When this happens, ask the person holding the envelope to tear it open and read the note aloud. *Ta dah!* You're a miracle worker!

- OK . . . but now you're wondering, "What if the volunteer *doesn't* choose that card?" The answer is "Make him choose it!" Here's how. Let's say the card chosen is the first one. When the volunteer touches that card, ask him to hand it to you. You put it aside. That leaves three cards on the table. Now ask your volunteer to pick two more cards. If the seven of hearts is not one of them, ask him to hand you those two cards, and place them near the  first card. You then say, "You have eliminated all but one card. That card is the seven of hearts." You then instruct the volunteer with the envelope to open it and read the note. It will match, of course.

- If, when you ask the volunteer to choose two more cards, one of them is the seven of hearts, say to him, "Hand me one of those cards— whichever you choose." If he hands you the seven of hearts, say, "The one you chose to hand me is the seven of hearts." The volunteer with the envelope is now told to open it. If the card he hands you is the *other* card, and he is still holding the seven of hearts, say, "The card you decided to keep is the seven of hearts." The volunteer with the envelope is now instructed to do her duty.

## FIRST-TIMER'S TIP!

**This trick is an absolute stunner when it's performed to perfection. Practice this trick so you'll remember how to guide your volunteer to the seven of hearts if it's not chosen right away. It must look like a free choice, *not* like you are forcing it.**

49

# The Genie of the Bottle

**TRICK: You prove that a genie lives in a bottle by sliding a rope into the bottle and commanding the genie to hold on to it. The genie does, and the bottle magically hangs on the end of the rope when you let go.**

## KEY WORD

suspension

## MATERIALS

- ball small enough to fit into the bottle

- bottle no more than 8 inches high (made of dark glass so you cannot see through it)

- piece of rope about 10 to 12 inches long

## GETTING READY

Before the trick begins, drop the ball into the bottle (this ball will act as your "genie").

## ON WITH THE SHOW!

Do this trick over a soft, flat surface so the bottle won't break if it falls.

**1.** "A genie lives in this bottle," you tell your audience, holding the bottle up. You then lower one end of the rope into the bottle. Keep feeding the rope into the bottle until the end of it reaches the bottom.

**2.** Stop here and, holding the rope in place with one hand and the bottle in the other, turn everything upside down. "Genie," you command, "hold on to the rope!"

**3.** Once the bottle is completely upside-down, tug gently on the end of the rope until you feel some resistance. What you are doing is wedging the ball between the rope and the neck of the bottle.

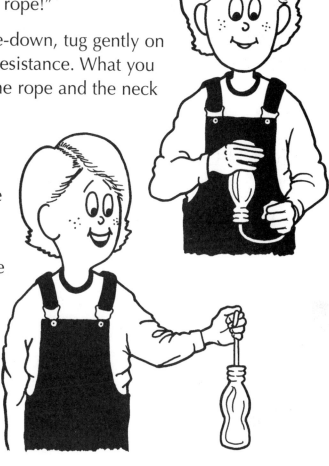

**4.** Let go of the rope. Because of the wedged ball, the rope stays in place. After a few seconds, grasp the end of the rope and turn the bottle right side up, then let go of the bottle. As you do, you command, "Don't let go, Genie." You are still holding on to the end of the rope with the other hand. The bottle will dangle safely on the other end! You tell your audience this is all the work of your "genie."

## FIRST-TIMER'S TIP!

If, at the end of the trick, someone asks to see the bottle and rope, you can do the following: Tip the bottle upside-down and grip it around the mouth. With your other hand, slowly pull the rope out of the bottle. The rope will pull the ball out of the bottle and into your hand holding the bottle. You can then hand around the bottle and rope to be examined while keeping the ball hidden in your hand.

# A Wand of a Different Color

## TRICK: You magically change the color of your magic wand to red.

### KEY WORDS

friction

transformation

### MATERIALS

- pencil
- ruler
- piece of wooden dowel about 12 inches long
- red paint
- paintbrush
- white paint
- black construction paper
- scissors
- clear tape
- single sheet of newspaper

## GETTING READY

**1.** First, you must make your magic wand. Lightly mark off 1½ inches on each end of the dowel. These will be the white tips of the wand.

**2.** With red paint, cover the middle of the wand (about 9 inches), and let dry overnight.

**3.** After the red paint has dried, cover the two ends with white paint. Again, let dry overnight. You now have a magic wand that is red with white tips.

**4.** Now cut a 9-inch-long strip from the black construction paper. Wrap this strip tightly around the middle of the wand so that it completely covers the red section, and tape it closed. The tape should only touch the construction paper, not your magic wand. With the construction paper tightly in place, the wand should appear normal.

## ON WITH THE SHOW!

**1.** Begin the trick by waving or twirling the wand a bit. No one will see the tape, and the paper should stay in place if it is wound tightly enough.

**2.** Now pick up the sheet of newspaper and begin to roll the wand inside it. Start at one end and roll the paper around the wand, making a long tube. Once the wand is completely wrapped, grip it around the middle with the fist of your nondominant hand.

**3.** With the flat palm of your other hand, push on one end of the wand and begin forcing it to the other end of the newspaper. (You may want to tap a bit on the one end to get it going in the right direction.) By forcing the wand out of the end of the newspaper, you are causing it to come out of its black construction paper covering. The construction paper will stay within the newspaper tube and the wand will appear red.

**4.** Once the wand has emerged from the end of the newspaper, the audience will see that the wand has "changed color." Finish by handing out the wand to be inspected—and crumpling up the newspaper to get rid of the evidence.

**left-handed example**

## FiRST-TiMER'S TiP!

It's a good idea to use the wand for a few tricks in your magic show before performing this one. That way your audience will have a chance to get used to seeing it as black and white—like any magic wand. They will not suspect a thing! When this trick is performed, their surprise will be even greater! They might then want to examine the wand. And why not? The construction paper is gone!

# The Ghost Handkerchief

**TRICK: An ordinary-looking handkerchief magically penetrates the bottom of a drinking glass.**

## KEY WORD
penetration

## MATERIALS

- white handkerchief

- drinking glass

- cloth such as a bandanna or women's scarf, or one of similar size (made of a fabric that is thick enough not to be seen through)

- rubber band

- table

## ON WITH THE SHOW!

**1.** Hold up the white handkerchief and explain, "Believe it or not, this handkerchief has many of the qualities of a ghost." Throw the handkerchief across the room, and say, "First of all, it can fly!"

**2.** Retrieve the handkerchief and continue: "Second, it can pass through solid objects!" You offer to demonstrate.

**3.** Pick up the glass with your dominant hand and stuff the handkerchief into it with your free hand. You must be holding the bottom of glass with your fingertips. Also make sure you pack the handkerchief into the glass so it stays near the bottom.

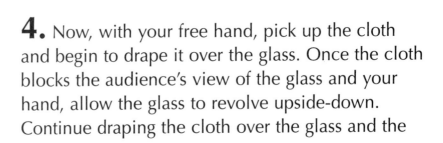

**right-handed example**

**4.** Now, with your free hand, pick up the cloth and begin to drape it over the glass. Once the cloth blocks the audience's view of the glass and your hand, allow the glass to revolve upside-down. Continue draping the cloth over the glass and the hand holding it, too. Your audience doesn't know it, but the cloth is actually being draped over the bottom of the glass.

**5.** Once the cloth has been draped, your free hand grips the glass through the cloth so your dominant hand can emerge from underneath and pick the rubber band up from the table.

**6.** That hand then wraps the rubber band around the cloth—and also around the bottom of the glass, though your audience thinks it has been placed around its mouth. They also think the handkerchief is sealed up inside.

**7.** You hold up the glass and announce, "Watch as the handkerchief penetrates the glass!" Reach up under the cloth and into the glass with your dominant hand and grip the handkerchief inside. Dramatically pull it out of the glass and toss it on the table!

**8.** Now reach back up underneath the cloth with the same hand and grip the mouth of the glass with your fingers. Your other hand grips the rubber band and cloth and pulls them off the glass, blocking the audience's view as the fingers gripping the glass revolve it back to the right-side-up position. When the cloth is removed, everything looks normal. Your audience is free to examine the glass, the handkerchief, and the cloth.

# Clever Card Counting

**TRICK: You read your volunteer's mind and name the card he "freely" chooses.**

## KEY WORDS

memory

mentalism

## MATERIALS

• deck of cards

• table

## GETTING READY

Before you begin the trick, you must secretly look at and remember the top card of the deck. This is the one your volunteer will end up with!

## ON WITH THE SHOW!

**1.** Begin the trick by telling your volunteer that you can name the card he will freely select. First, ask him to choose a number between 1 and 10.

**2.** When your volunteer calls out a number, you "demonstrate" how you want the cards dealt out. Let's say the number chosen is 6. Look at your volunteer. "I want you to deal out six cards in a nice neat pile like this," you say as you deal six cards off the top of the deck. "Stop dealing when you get to your number." Now let's look at what just happened. The first card you dealt to the table was the card you memorized. You then dealt five more cards on top of it. Your memorized card is now on the bottom of the pile.

**3.** Now pick up that pile and place it back on top of the deck. Hand the deck to your volunteer and tell him to deal to his selected

56

number. As the volunteer deals that number, the six cards you removed and then replaced are being dealt backward—right to your memorized card! The last card he deals will be that card.

**4.** Ask your volunteer to look at the last card dealt; then have fun "reading" his mind!

# BRAIN BUSTER

How could this trick be done with a bigger number? "Demonstrating" how to deal the cards if your volunteer chooses a number like 18 would take forever! People will lose interest by the time you finish. Here's a way to do a similar trick using numbers between 10 and 20, with your volunteer doing all the dealing. You never have to touch the cards! Secretly memorize the 10th card down from the top of the deck. Have your volunteer think of a number between 10 and 20. Tell him to deal that many cards into a pile. Now ask him to add together the two digits that make up his chosen number. In other words, if your volunteer chooses 16, then the numbers 1 and 6 are added together to get 7. Whatever the number turns out to be, have him deal that many cards off of the pile he's just dealt. When the last card is dealt, tell him to look at that card. It will be the card you memorized! Try it yourself.

## FIRST-TIMER'S TIP!

As with all mentalism tricks, you should take your time "reading" your volunteer's thoughts. Don't just come right out and name the card. Identify the color first. Then say whether it is a low or high number. Stare into his eyes as if you are trying to really pull his thoughts out of his mind. Finally, name the card. All of this builds up suspense and is more fun than naming the card right off the bat!

# The Box of Tricks

**TRICK: You magically produce a number of things from inside an apparently empty box.**

## KEY WORD
production

## MATERIALS

- scissors
- heavy thread
- needle
- cloth bag, sewn by an adult (The bag should easily fit into the box.)
- empty shoebox with lid
- small objects, like candy or toys, all able to fit into the cloth bag

## GETTING READY

**1.** Cut two identical lengths of heavy thread and sew them to the corners of the bag.

**2.** Attach the other ends of the thread to the box lid. Make two very small holes in one of the long folds. Then tie the ends of the thread through these holes. The exact length of thread must be experimented with, but the idea is to hide the bag behind the lid of the box so it won't be seen by the audience.

**3.** Now fill the bag with the candy or other small objects. Make sure they all stay in the bag.

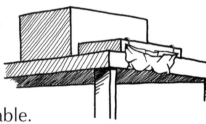

**4.** Put the box on the table, and place the lid behind it. The inside of the lid must be facing up. The bag hangs over the edge of the table.

## ON WITH THE SHOW!

**1.** Tell the audience, "I once visited a very special candy store. The owner was a magician." After a pause, you say, "When I walked into the store, it was completely empty." Show that the box is empty by tilting it toward the audience and placing your hand inside. Then put the box back where it was.

58

**2.** Now pick up the lid with both hands, tilting it so the inside of the lid faces the audience. (If this is done properly, the bag will not be seen as it moves from the edge of the table to the back of the lid. Of course, this must be practiced until you get the timing right.)

**3.** Now you say, "The owner told me there was candy everywhere—I just had to believe." After showing the lid, lower it toward and slightly in front of the box. As you do this, the bag should lower into the box.

**4.** Once the bag reaches the inside of the box, revolve the lid (so the inside moves toward you as you turn it over), then place it on top of the box. To the audience it will appear that you are merely showing both the box and lid to be empty before closing the box.

**5.** "So I closed my eyes," you continue, "and pictured the candy that was supposed to be there. When I opened my eyes . . . there was candy everywhere I looked!" Wave your hands over the closed box. Open it by lifting the side of the lid closest to you straight up and then away from you. Hold the lid in this position, and with your other hand, reach into the bag and take out all the candy from it. It will look as if these things appeared from nowhere! Hand the candy out for your audience to enjoy.

# Threading a Needle by Magic

**TRICK: Demonstrating with a piece of rope, you show how you solve the problem of threading a needle by using magic.**

## KEY WORD
penetration

## MATERIALS

- piece of thin rope about 3 feet long

## ON WITH THE SHOW!

**1.** "Have you ever tried threading a needle?" you ask your audience. "It is a pain! You have to squint and try to get the end of the thread through that tiny hole in the needle. After 20 minutes, if you're lucky and you haven't stuck yourself, you finally get it threaded."

**2.** You pick up the piece of rope with your dominant hand. "Well," you continue, "I've found an easier way to thread a needle using magic. Let me show you." Drape the rope over the thumb of your opposite hand. The end of the rope hanging farthest from your body should be shorter by about 12 inches than the end closest to you.

**3.** Take the longer end and begin winding it around your thumb. You must wind the rope away from you and around the back of your thumb.

**right-handed example**

60

**4.** After a few winds around the thumb, form the rope into a loop and hold this loop in place with your thumb and fingers.

**5.** Call your audience's attention to the loop. "For my demonstration, this will be the eye of the needle," you tell them.

**6.** Now pick up the other end of the rope in your free hand. "This will be the thread," you explain. Then you say, "When you have magic on your side, everything becomes just a little easier. Watch!" Holding the rope between your fingers and thumb, "aim" the end toward the loop.

**7.** Now make a quick jabbing motion with the end of your "thread" toward the loop. You miss it completely, but as you pass the loop, you allow it to loosen a little in your thumb and fingers. At the same time, the hand holding the "thread" pulls tight on its end. This will cause one of the winds of rope to slip off the thumb and through the loop. It will appear as if you magically threaded the "eye" by causing the rope to penetrate the loop!

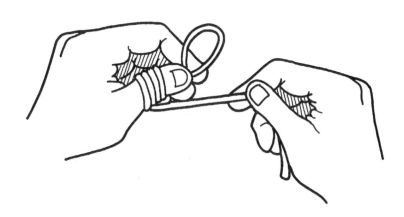

**8.** "Unthread" the "eye" by pulling the piece of rope back out of the loop. This trick can be repeated as long as there are wraps of rope on your thumb.

# The Escaping and Nonescaping Rubber Band

**TRICK: You magically "free" a rubber band from your fingers, while a volunteer cannot.**

## KEY WORDS

"betcha"

rubber

## MATERIALS

• rubber band

## ON WITH THE SHOW!

**1.** Begin by showing the rubber band and looping it around the index fingers of both hands. Point the left finger to the right with the right finger pointed to the left just below it. The rubber band forms a simple loop around the two fingers.

**2.** Begin twirling your fingers around each other, moving the band in circles.

**3.** After a few twirls, stop so that your fingers change position: The left finger is now on the bottom, and the right finger is now on top.

**4.** Now touch the right index finger and thumb together and the left index finger and thumb together.

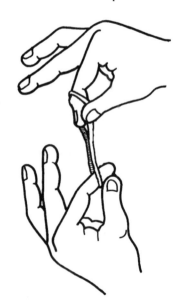

**5.** Keeping your fingers in this position, the right hand moves toward your body while you twist your wrist so the open fingers point downward. At the same time, move your left hand away from it.

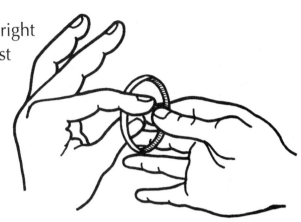

**6.** Now bring your hands in toward each other. Touch the tip of each index finger to the tip of the opposite thumb.

**7.** Now, keeping them together, stretch open your fingers. Your right index finger and left thumb move downward and your left index finger and right thumb move upward. The rubber band should now freely fall to the floor.

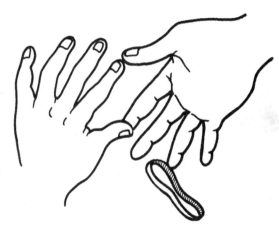

**8.** Hand the rubber band to someone from the audience and challenge her to duplicate your feat. Chances are, she will forget to rotate her hands away from each other (Step 5) and will therefore end up getting the rubber band tangled in her fingers!

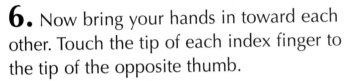

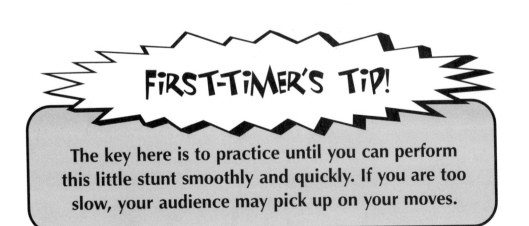

# FiRST-TiMER'S TiP!

**The key here is to practice until you can perform this little stunt smoothly and quickly. If you are too slow, your audience may pick up on your moves.**

# The Thumb of the Human Pincushion

**TRICK: You tell your audience about a visit you made recently to the carnival, where you witnessed the Human Pincushion sticking pins into his thumb. To illustrate, you stick pins into your own thumb!**

## KEY WORD

penetration

## MATERIALS

- small piece of carrot (Peeled baby carrots work perfectly.)

- handkerchief

- table

- four or five straight pins

**NOTE:** You are not actually sticking pins into your thumb. Instead, they are being stuck into the carrot.

## GETTING READY

Hide the carrot in the fist of your nondominant hand. If you are standing while doing this trick, you can turn slightly so your opposite side faces the audience. If you are sitting, just rest the fist in your lap.

## ON WITH THE SHOW!

**1.** Begin by telling your audience about a carnival you visited recently. "I went into one of those oddity shows," you tell them. "You know, where they display things like the world's biggest cow, from whose leg you can make 125 hamburgers, or the 40-foot-long snake that has only one fang, so it hisses with a lisp."

**2.** "Well," you continue, "what I found most interesting was the Human Pincushion. This is what he did." Pick up the handkerchief from the table with your dominant hand. At the same

**right-handed example**

time, bring your opposite hand into view, still in a fist but with your thumb extended. "He stuck his thumb up," you explain, "and covered it with a cloth, like this." Start to cover your thumb with the handkerchief. Once the handkerchief blocks your audience's view of your thumb, lower the thumb and push the carrot up into place. Then drape the handkerchief over the carrot.

**3.** Continue with your story. "Then he started sticking pins in his thumb!" Pick up one of the pins and stick it through the handkerchief partway into the carrot. Let some of the pin stick out. Pause for a moment so your audience can clearly see the pin sticking out of your "thumb."

**4.** Continue sticking pins into the carrot. Say, "He stuck each pin he had there right into his thumb!" Let the audience see your "thumb" for a few seconds, with all the pins sticking out of it.

**5.** Now begin to remove the pins one by one, until all are out and back on the table. With your free hand, remove the handkerchief, taking the carrot with it as you do. At the same moment, stick your thumb back up into the air so the audience sees it when the handkerchief is removed. It will look as if it was sticking up the entire time! Say to your audience, "And the pins left no marks in his thumb at all. It was absolutely amazing!"

**SAFETY FIRST**

Be careful when handling the straight pins.

# Calculating at Lightning Speed

## TRICK: You demonstrate how you can add numbers in your head faster than they can be added on a calculator.

### KEY WORDS
calculator

mentalism

### MATERIALS
- pencil
- pad of paper
- calculator

## ON WITH THE SHOW!

**1.** "I am able to do math at an incredible speed," you tell your audience. "I am faster than most calculators." You offer to demonstrate.

**2.** Ask an audience member to call out a five-digit number. Any number will work. Write it at the top of the pad.

**3.** Ask another spectator to call out another five-digit number, and write it on the pad underneath the first number.

**4.** At this point you choose a number yourself. Each digit of the five-digit number you write down must add up to 9 when added to the digit just above it.

**5.** A third volunteer is asked to call out a five-digit number, and you write it down underneath the number you chose.

**6.** Again you choose a five-digit number, and again each digit must add up to 9 when added to the digit just above it. You now have a list of five 5-digit numbers. Draw a line underneath, and also draw a + sign to the left of the bottom number.

75,733
21,060
78,939
11,234
+ 88,765
275,731

66

**7.** Show the pad to the audience, so they can see that all the numbers written there are in fact the ones called out. Hand a calculator to a volunteer. "You and I will race to see who can do the math and come up with the correct total first," you say to your volunteer.

**8.** You say, "Go," and your volunteer starts entering the numbers. All you have to do is subtract 2 from the last digit in the number at the top of the pad, and then add 2 to the front of the number!

**9.** Write down your total on the pad as soon as you have figured it out. Your audience, as well as the person operating the calculator, will be amazed at how fast you did the math in your head. Tell the person with the calculator to continue, to make sure you are correct. Of course you are, and your audience will be even more amazed at that!

## FIRST-TIMER'S TIP!

This trick can be repeated with different numbers and a different total. Do not repeat it a third time, however. Some people in the audience may start picking up on patterns that appear in the figures. After you've performed the trick twice, act as if you are tired—calculating all those figures so fast took a lot out of you! Offer to perform your amazing feats of calculation another day.

# Cowboy Magic

**TRICK: You demonstrate your skill as a cowboy when you magically "rope" the end of your bandanna.**

## KEY WORDS

cowboy

Old West

production

## GETTING READY

To prepare for this trick, tie a knot in one corner of the bandanna. Hold the bandanna by this corner so the knot is hidden in your dominant hand.

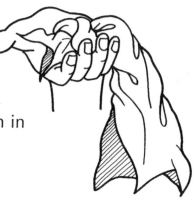

## MATERIALS

• bandanna

## ON WITH THE SHOW!

**1.** Start by holding the bandanna as described. Explain how you've always liked reading about cowboys and the Old West. Offer to demonstrate your skill as a cowboy.

**2.** With your free hand, grab the end of the bandanna that's hanging and place it in your opposite hand so it now forms a loop around your hand.

**3.** Quickly shake out the bandanna, releasing the end you just put there.

**right-handed example**

**4.** Grab the end of the bandanna and place it in your hand, as before.

**5.** Shake the bandanna out again, and again let go of the same end.

**6.** Once again, place the end of the bandanna in your hand. Shout out one good "Yee-ha!" and shake out the bandanna again, but this time release the knotted end of the bandanna. You are now holding on to the unknotted end. It looks as if the knot magically appeared!

# The Ring in the Tea Bag

**TRICK: You call out a magic word, and a ring vanishes—until you cause it to reappear inside a tea bag.**

## KEY WORDS

transposition

vanish

## MATERIALS

- finger ring (The ring should not be too big. The thinner or smaller, the better.)

- handkerchief

- tea bag (one with a paper tab)

- table

## ON WITH THE SHOW!

**1.** Borrow a finger ring from a volunteer. Hold the ring upright at the fingertips of your dominant hand. With your other hand, cover both the ring and hand with the handkerchief.

**2.** Once the handkerchief is in place, your now free (dominant) hand moves to grip the ring through the cloth of the handkerchief. As that hand reaches the ring, your hand (underneath the handkerchief) allows the ring to slip down to the base of the fingers, where it is held loosely in place. The hand gripping the center of the handkerchief as if holding the ring moves away from the hand underneath. That hand drops to your side, the fingers curled slightly to keep the ring in place. (The hand should not be closed in a fist. Instead, it should appear to be empty to anyone who might look at it.) You are, meanwhile, looking at and therefore directing attention to your opposite hand, which apparently holds the ring.

**right-handed example**

70

**3.** Using the hand whose fingers hide the ring, pick up the tea bag by its paper tab and hand it to another volunteer. You should pick up the paper tab between your thumb and index finger. This will allow the rest of your fingers to close into a fist, hiding the ring, and still look natural.

**4.** Once the volunteer is holding the tea bag by the tab, your now free hand (except for the hidden ring!) grips the handkerchief between the thumb and index finger, just as with the tea bag. That hand whips the cloth off the opposite hand to show the ring has "vanished"!

**5.** Drop the handkerchief to the table and immediately take the tea bag from the volunteer holding it. Grip the bag between the fingers and thumbs of both hands in preparation to tear it open. The fingers of the hand *not* holding the ring should be gripping the top end of the bag.

**6.** That hand then tears off the top of the tea bag and drops that piece to the table. Take the now open bag in the same hand and begin to pour the leaves out into the opposite palm. As you do this, aim the bag so the leaves are poured directly on top of the hidden ring.

**7.** Once the bag is empty, drop it to the table and begin to sift through the tea leaves until the ring is exposed. It will look as if the ring magically flew to the tea bag! An absolute miracle!

# BRAIN BUSTER

This trick is based on an idea by an ingenious close-up magician named Bill Goodwin: A marked coin penetrates a sugar packet a couple of times and then ends up sealed inside the packet. See if you can come up with similar ideas, making borrowed or marked objects disappear and then magically reappear elsewhere.

# The Deck Knows!

**TRICK: Your deck of cards magically produces your volunteer's most favorite card—making it pop right out of the deck!**

## KEY WORDS

force

pressure

production

## MATERIALS

- deck of cards, with card box
- table

## ON WITH THE SHOW!

**1.** Hand the deck of cards to a volunteer and ask her to pull out three favorite cards.

**2.** Once the three cards are on the table, ask your volunteer to look them over and pick out her favorite of the three.

**3.** You then fan out the cards in your nondominant hand so most of the faces can be seen. Pick up one of the favorites from the table—not the *most* favorite but one of the other two. Insert this card into the fan, near the middle. Let about half of it stick out of the fan.

**4.** Now pick up the most favorite card and insert it, too, about halfway into the fan, one card over to the right of the first card you put in. In other words, one of the favorites and the most favorite should be sticking out about halfway, with one card in between them.

**5.** Pick up the final card from the table and insert it to the right of the most favorite card, leaving one card in between, just as before. All three favorite cards should be sticking about halfway out of the deck.

**left-handed example**

**6.** Carefully close the fan and insert the deck into the card box. (The deck should go in only about halfway.) The deck should be held together as you do this, and the three extended cards should remain in place. Hold the entire set of cards in place by squeezing the sides of the box.

**7.** Hold the box (in your nondominant hand) so the faces of the cards are facing the audience. With your opposite index finger, push the three favorite cards down so they become flush with the rest of the deck.

**8.** Say to your volunteer, "We all know what your favorite card is, but does the deck know?" After saying this, release the pressure on the sides of the card box and allow the cards to fall all the way into the box. They will all fall into the case except the most favorite card! It will be sticking out of the deck. The deck knows!

## BRAIN BUSTER

What is it that makes the volunteer's most favorite card stick out of the deck? To find out, try doing the trick without the box (and without an audience!). Hold on to the sides of the deck as if it were in the box and you were squeezing the sides to hold it in place. Push down on the three favorite cards and watch the bottom of the deck as you do. What is happening? Now sharply strike the bottom of the deck against a table, as if you'd dropped the cards into the box. When you do this, watch the top of the deck. What happens now? After doing this little experiment, you should have a better understanding of how the most favorite card pops out of the deck.

73

# "Shear" Rope Magic

## TRICK: You magically fuse two pieces of rope back into one.

### KEY WORDS
fusion

restoration

### MATERIALS

- scissors
- ruler
- length of thin rope about 3 feet long
- table

## GETTING READY

**1.** Before the trick begins, cut off one end of the rope. The piece you cut off should measure approximately 4 inches.

**2.** Fold this piece of rope in half and hold it secretly in your dominant hand. The long piece of rope should be held by its end in your other hand. The scissors are nearby on the table.

## ON WITH THE SHOW!

**1.** Begin the trick by showing the audience the long piece of rope. The hand hiding the small piece of rope reaches over and grabs the middle of the piece you're showing. (The hidden piece is held flat against this middle section of rope.) The hand holding the end of the long piece lets go so the rope now drapes from your dominant hand.

**right-handed example**

**2.** Your free hand grips the rope at the spot where it is being held. As that hand grips the rope, it covers the tips of your dominant hand. The dominant hand now pulls the small piece of rope upward so it emerges from the top of the other hand. The small piece is then held in a loop in the fist of that other hand. The rest of the long piece of rope is below that hand, hanging toward the floor. At this point, the illusion is that the middle of the rope is being held, while the rest of the rope hangs down. However, what the audience is really seeing is the "secret" piece of rope, *not* the true middle of the long piece.

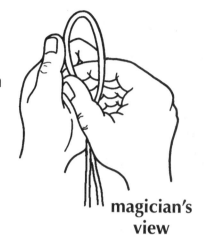

**magician's view**

**3.** Pick the scissors up in your dominant hand and begin to cut the secret piece in half. When that is done, continue to snip little bits until that piece has all been cut up. To the audience, it will look as if you cut the long piece of rope in half. And you have just destroyed the evidence to the contrary!

**4.** Put the scissors back down, and clasp the long piece of rope in the middle between your hands. Roll your hands back and forth and tell the audience that you are fusing the rope back together.

**5.** Open your hands to show the rope back in one piece.

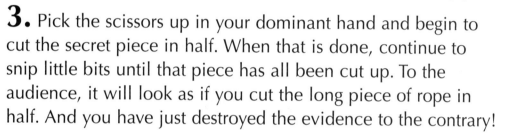

# FIRST-TIMER'S TIP!

In the trick described here, the hidden, folded piece of rope measures about 4 inches. Of course, all hands are different, and a 4-inch piece of rope may be too big for you to secretly hold. Experiment with different sizes until you find the one that is right for you.

75

# Where to Find More Magic

## MAGIC MAGAZINES

If you are interested in learning more about the art of magic, there are a few magazines you can check out. These will not be found in your local bookstore or newsstand. They can be found, however, in magic shops. Or, with a parent's permission, you can subscribe to them and have them come straight to your home.

*M A G I C:* The Independent Magazine for Magicians
7380 S. Eastern Avenue, Suite 124-179
Las Vegas, NV 89123

*Genii* Magazine
4200 Wisconsin Avenue, NW, Suite 106-384
Washington, DC 20016

Both of these magazines contain the newest tricks in the field, feature articles, and the latest news on magic and magicians. They also have lots of ads from magic shops around the world.

## MAGIC SHOPS

Listed below are a few magic shops located across the country. These are good places to get started in magic. Why? Because they have all the stuff you need! All of these shops have magic books, magazines, props, and the newest tricks out on the market today. Most will send you a catalog. Most of these shops have toll-free phone numbers that are used for orders only. If you should have questions about anything you see in a catalog, please do not use the toll-free line. Use the regular phone number instead. And you should always get your parents' permission before you call any of these magic shops.

Brad Burt's Magic Shop
4204 Convoy Street
San Diego, CA 92111
Phone orders only: (800) 748-5759
Help & information line: (619) 571-4749
Web site: www.magicshop.com

H & R Magic Books
3839 Liles Lane
Humble, TX 77396-4088
Phone: (281) 454-7219
Web site: www.magicbookshop.com

Hank Lee's Magic Factory
Mail Order Division
P.O. Box 789
Medford, MA 02155
Phone orders only: (800) 874-7400
Help & information line: (617) 482-8749 or (617) 482-8750
Web site: www.hanklee.com or allmagic.com/magicfactory

Hollywood Magic, Inc.
6614 Hollywood Boulevard
Hollywood, CA 90028
Phone: (323) 464-5610

Louis Tannen, Inc.
24 West 25th Street
2nd Floor
New York, NY 10010
Phone orders only: (800) 72-MAGIC
Help & information line: (212) 929-4500
Web site: www.tannenmagic.com

## MAGIC ORGANIZATIONS

There are magicians' organizations around the world that you can join to learn more about the art of magic. Most organizations have local chapters that meet usually once a month. Members who attend these meetings include magicians of all ages. They all enjoy the hobby of magic and share secrets with one another. Conventions where some of the top names in magic come to perform are held usually once a year.

If this sounds like fun to you, contact one or both of the organizations listed below. They will be happy to tell you where the nearest chapter is for you to attend meetings, how much the dues are, and other information.

International Brotherhood of Magicians
11137C South Towne Square
St. Louis, MO 63123-7819
*Junior members must be at least 12 years old. All members receive a monthly magic magazine,* The Linking Ring. *There are over 300 chapters (called Rings) worldwide.*

Society of American Magicians
P.O. Box 510260
St. Louis, MO 63151
Phone: (888) 726-9644
E-mail: hardinjo@htc.net
*This is the oldest magical society in the world. Houdini was the society's national president until his death. Members receive a monthly magic magazine, M-U-M. There are over 250 chapters (called Assemblies) worldwide.*

*Contact the Society of American Magicians (SAM) and ask about their Society of Young Magicians program. SYM is an organization specifically for young people that is part of SAM. It was founded in 1984 by five members of the SAM as a way of encouraging kids between the ages of 7 and 17 to take up magic as a hobby. Members receive their own newsletter, called the Magic SYMbol. Many SAM Assemblies allow SYM members to participate in their activities.*

# Glossary of Magic Terms

The words that follow are terms that you should be familiar with if you decide to take up magic as a hobby. Some of the terms listed here are in this book; some are not. However, the terms not found in this book will be words that you will discover early on as you read and learn more about magic.

**close-up magic:** A style of magic that can be performed at a close distance, usually at a table or in a spectator's hands.

**cut:** Rearranging the order of a deck of cards by removing about half the deck from the top and placing it to one side, then taking what's left of the deck and putting it on top of the portion you've just removed.

**effect:** Another name for the trick being performed. The effect is what the audience sees.

**fan:** An action performed with a deck of cards. The cards, held in one hand, are spread out in a formation resembling a fan so that all the faces and/or backs can be seen.

**force:** To cause someone to select a card or object you want them to select, while creating the impression they actually have a choice.

**mentalism:** The area of magic dealing with tricks of the mind (mind reading, fortune-telling, telepathy, etc.).

**method:** Another word for the secret to a magic trick. The method is how the trick is done.

**misdirection:** The technique of averting your spectators' attention away from the secret of the trick by using your eyes, actions, or words.

**palming:** The action of secretly hiding an object in your hand without the audience's knowledge.

**parlor magic:** A style of magic performed in the parlors of earlier times. Today it is performed at fairly close distance in a room or on a platform. It is performed much closer than stage magic, yet not quite as close as close-up magic.

**prestidigitation:** Another word for *sleight of hand.*

**sleight of hand:** A magic trick that requires skilled use of one's hands. Most close-up magic tricks require sleight of hand.

**spectator:** One who watches a magic trick. Every member of the audience is a spectator.

# Index

## A
air pressure, 34–35
asymmetry, 26

## B
balancing tricks, 34–35
bandanna tricks,
    30–31, 68–69

## C
cards, playing
    mentalism tricks,
        18–19, 26–27,
        32–33, 48–49,
        56–57
    production tricks,
        72–73
    transformation tricks,
        46–47
clairvoyance, 15
close-up magic, 7, 79
coin tricks, vanishing,
    28–29, 36–37
costumes, 10–11
counting cards, 56–57
cutting, card, 79

## D
diffusion tricks, 40–42
disappearing tricks
    coins, 28–29, 36–37
    ring, 70–71
dollar bill tricks,
    34–35,        38–39

## E
energy, 43–44
escaping tricks, 62–63
ESP, 15

## F
fanning, card, 79
force, 72–73, 79
fortune-telling, 79
    See also mentalism
        tricks
friction, 52–53
fusion, 74–75

## G
gravitation, 18–19

## H
handkerchief tricks,
    54–55, 70–71
hat trick, 18–19
human pincushion
    trick, 64–65

## M
magazines, magic, 76
magician's costume,
    10–11
magic rules, 13–14
magic shops, 76–77
magic wand trick,
    52–53
memorization tricks,
    16–17, 56–57
mentalism tricks
    calculating numbers,
        66–67
    cards, playing,
        26–27, 32–33,
        48–49, 56–57
    memorization,
        16–17
mind reading, 15, 79
mind reading tricks,
    15, 56–57

misdirection, 12–13,
    79
momentum, 28–29
money tricks. See
    coin tricks; dollar
    bill tricks

## O
optical illusions,
    20–21,        38–39
organizations, magic,
    77–78

## P
palming, 79
parlor magic, 7–8, 79
penetration tricks
    glass, 54–55
    human pincushion,
        64–65
    rope, 60–61
    solid objects, 22–23
pressure, 72–73
production tricks
    cards, playing,
        72–73
    empty box, 43–45,
        58–59
    rope, 68–69

## R
reappearing tricks,
    28–29, 70–71
rehearsal, 11–12
restoration tricks,
    74–75
rope tricks, 50–51,
    60–61, 74–75
rubber band trick,
    62–63
rules, magic, 13–14

## S
salt shaker trick, 22–23
sleight of hand, 79
solid objects, 22–23
spectator, 79
stage magic, 7–8
straw trick, 24–25
suspension tricks,
    34–35, 50–51
symmetry, 26–27

## T
telepathy, 79
    See also mentalism
        tricks
transformation tricks
    bandanna, 30–31
    cards, playing,
        46–47
    magic wand, 52–53
    water, 40–42
transposition tricks,
    70–71

## V
vanishing tricks, 28–29,
    36–37